THE
UNBREAKABLE
MARRIAGE

HOW TO STAND IN UNITY AND WITHSTAND ADVERSITY

WORKBOOK

JEEVA AND SULOJANA SAM

THE UNBREAKABLE MARRIAGE WORKBOOK

Copyright © 2022 Jeeva and Sulojana Sam

ISBN: 978-1-7780861-3-7

All rights reserved. Except for brief excerpts for review purposes, no part of this book may be reproduced or used in any form or media without permission from the publisher.

Any website addresses recommended throughout this book are offered as a resource to you. These websites are not intended in any way to imply an endorsement from the authors, nor do they vouch for their content. The information in this book was correct at the time it was published.

All Scripture quotations, unless otherwise indicated, are taken from the Holy Bible, New International Version®, NIV®. Copyright ©1973, 1978, 1984, 2011 by Biblica, Inc.™ Used by permission of Zondervan. All rights reserved worldwide. www.zondervan.com. The "NIV" and "New International Version" are trademarks registered in the United States Patent and Trademark Office by Biblica, Inc.™

Scripture quotations marked NLT are taken from the Holy Bible, New Living Translation, copyright ©1996, 2004, 2015 by Tyndale House Foundation. Used by permission of Tyndale House Publishers, a Division of Tyndale House Ministries, Carol Stream, Illinois 60188. All rights reserved.

Scripture quotations marked TPT are from The Passion Translation®. Copyright © 2017, 2018 by Passion & Fire Ministries, Inc. Used by permission. All rights reserved. ThePassionTranslation.com.

Scripture quotations marked GNT are taken from the Good News Translation - Second Edition © 1992 by American Bible Society. Used by permission.

Cover design by Hester Barnard. Graphic inspired by a vision God gave Steven Kasyanenko.
All other graphics and typesetting by Krysta Koppel, Engage Communication Co.

CONTENTS

A Message from the Sams........................5

Chapter 1: Fundamental Principles 7

Chapter 2: Assessing Your Marriage..............13

Chapter 3: Shifting The Spiritual Atmosphere 19

Chapter 4: Removing Spiritual Blockages.............33

Chapter 5: Growing In Communication 49

Chapter 6: Restoring Peace Following Conflict 61

Chapter 7: Going Undercovers 69

Chapter 8: Making Time...............................77

Chapter 9: Marital Finances...........................83

Chapter 10: Boundaries................................91

Celebrate Your Unbreakable Marriage..................97

A Blessing For Your Marriage 99

Where Do You Go From Here? 101

Accountability Tracker...............................103

A MESSAGE FROM THE SAMS

This workbook is designed specifically for couples who have decided to put into action the principles, strategies and steps that are found in our book *The Unbreakable Marriage*.

When you diligently follow what we share in the following pages, you are positioning yourselves to experience a breakthrough in your marriage as other couples have, often in as little as 10 weeks.

No matter where you're at right now--

- Facing a marriage breakdown or separated and considering divorce,
- Not at the breaking point, but realizing that unless you do something right now, you are headed for a breakdown,
- Newly married or engaged, needing a strong foundation and framework to build a marriage that lasts "till death do us part"--

The resources in this workbook will produce results for you as long as you meet one condition: BOTH of you, husband *and* wife are willing to work together through them.

For maximum results, we highly recommend that you find yourself a mentoring couple who will keep you accountable as you go through this process. It could be someone in your church, family or friendship circles that has been married longer (at least 5 years) and is willing to stick with you for a minimum of 10-12 weeks. Accountability is one of the keys that allows us to guarantee results for the couples we mentor. You will find that this is true for you as well.

****We also recognize that some of you are in such bad shape that you cannot work on these steps together as a couple right now. There is too much hurt, too much drama and too much conflict for you to overcome on your own. And there is too little communication, intimacy, trust or goodwill between the two of you.

You will need expert help to take you from breakdown to breakthrough.

This is why we offer personalized, customized mentorship. Please go to www.thesams.ca and submit your application. We will follow up with a free consultation and design a plan of action suited exclusively to address your unique situation.****

Thank you for choosing to get your hands on this companion workbook to *The Unbreakable Marriage*. Our prayers are with you as you embark on your journey to a Christ-centered, Holy Spirit-led marriage marked by lasting love, joy and peace.

Jeeva and Sulojana Sam

P.S: We invite you to join an exclusive Facebook Group called "The Unbreakable Marriage Community" where you can ask questions, share your progress and access bonus materials we will provide from time to time. Just click on: https://www.facebook.com/groups/theunbreakablemarriage/ or scan the QR code below:

CHAPTER 1

FUNDAMENTAL PRINCIPLES

CHAPTER 1: FUNDAMENTAL PRINCIPLES

YOU HAVE NO "MARRIAGE PROBLEMS"

"You have no marriage problems. You are two individuals with your own problems coupled together in a marriage." - Jeeva and Sulojana Sam

What unhealed hurts or unmet needs might you have brought with you when you got married?

_____

_____

_____

_____

How do you think these hurts affected your marriage?

_____

_____

_____

_____

_____

THE SPIRIT-SOUL-BODY CONNECTION

*"Now may the God of peace make you holy in every way, and may your whole **spirit** and **soul** and **body** be kept blameless until our Lord Jesus Christ comes again"*
(1 Thessalonians 5:23 NLT emphasis ours).

"For a marriage to be restored fully, we need to be aware that we are **spirit** beings with a **soul** in a **body**."
- Jeeva and Sulojana Sam

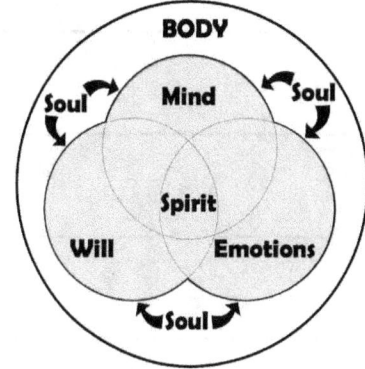

Why is the spirit-soul-body connection important for your marriage?

_____

_____

_____

_____

_____

_____

_____

CHAPTER 1: FUNDAMENTAL PRINCIPLES

As you read the illustration of this connection in the book, can you think of any instances in your own marriage where:

a. You took all three realms into consideration? How did that turn out?

_____

_____

_____

_____

b. You have tried to resolve something without taking all three realms into consideration? How did that turn out?

_____

_____

_____

_____

CHAPTER 1: FUNDAMENTAL PRINCIPLES

"MEN ARE LIKE WAFFLES, WOMEN ARE LIKE SPAGHETTI"

What differences are you aware of that exist between the two of you because one is female, and one is male?

_____

_____

_____

_____

_____

How have these differences affected the way you interact with each other, both positively and negatively?

_____

_____

_____

_____

CHAPTER 1: FUNDAMENTAL PRINCIPLES

NOTES

CHAPTER 2

ASSESSING YOUR MARRIAGE

ASSESSMENT #1: THE PREPARE-ENRICH INVENTORY

Complete the assessment on www.prepare-enrich.com or www.couplecheckup.com.

Based on the results of your assessment:

1. What in the report was not a surprise? i.e. areas that you would have classified as strengths and growth areas in your marriage anyway?

_____

_____

_____

_____

2. What in the report surprised/shocked you? i.e. what you thought were strengths being classified as growth areas and vice versa? Why might this be the case?

_____

_____

_____

_____

CHAPTER 2: ASSESSING YOUR MARRIAGE

ASSESSMENT #2: THE LOVE LANGUAGES QUIZ

Take the free quiz at www.5lovelanguages.com/quizzes/couples-quiz.

What are my primary love languages?

_____

_____

Complete this sentence: I feel most loved when…

_____

_____

_____

What are my spouse's primary love languages?

_____

_____

Complete this sentence: I can help my spouse feel most loved by…

_____

_____

_____

CHAPTER 2: ASSESSING YOUR MARRIAGE

What did you learn about each other's love languages after sharing your responses to these questions?

_____

_____

_____

_____

_____

For deeper study, we highly recommend you read Dr. Gary Chapman's book, *Five Love Languages*, to understand each other better.

CHAPTER 2: ASSESSING YOUR MARRIAGE

NOTES

CHAPTER 2: ASSESSING YOUR MARRIAGE

NOTES

CHAPTER 3

SHIFTING THE SPIRITUAL ATMOSPHERE

CHAPTER 3: SHIFTING THE SPIRITUAL ATMOSPHERE

> "The key to shifting the spiritual atmosphere is not complicated at all. It is as simple as developing certain daily spiritual habits, and practicing them regularly, consistently, and persistently. Spiritual habits sustain Holy Spirit habitation."
> - Jeeva and Sulojana Sam

Sow a thought, reap an action; sow an action, reap a habit; sow a habit, reap a character; sow a character, reap a destiny.
- Ralph Waldo Emerson

DAILY SPIRITUAL HABITS

1. SOAKING

"Be still and know that I am God" (Psalm 46:10).

Soaking is a time to simply spend quiet time with God.

- Set aside a block of time where you are totally free from distractions.

- Turn off your phones. Silence all the noises that would normally bombard your senses, e.g. TV, computer, etc. If you have children, find a time when they are safe or asleep.

- Keep a pen and paper (preferably a notebook/journal) beside you.

- Put yourself in a relaxing position. (Lying down is best, in our experience). Close your eyes.

- Say this simple prayer: "Holy Spirit, come!"

- Stay still and WAIT. Don't pray. Don't read. Just be quiet and still.

- If you do receive any revelations, write them down.

- Above all, be transformed by simply being in His Presence.

Many people find music can help with soaking. Find something peaceful and instrumental. Soak for a minimum 15 minutes/day, separately or together.

What pieces of music (if any) do you find the most helpful for soaking?

_____

_____

_____

_____

2. PRAISE AND WORSHIP

"Yet you are holy, enthroned on the praises of Israel" (Psalm 22:3).

A wealth of praise and worship music can be found on YouTube or your favourite music app. Lyrics are often available online, sometimes embedded in music videos directly.

Build your own playlist with songs that help you praise and worship God.

You can also use CDs and DVDs if you do not have access to online resources.

Who are some worship leaders/groups that you find most helpful to enter into God's Presence?

_____

_____

_____

_____

3. GRATITUDE

> *"Give thanks in all circumstances; for this is God's will for you in Christ Jesus"*
> (1 Thessalonians 5:18).

Start a "Gratitude Journal" and make two specific entries every day by answering these two questions:

1. What am I thankful for today?
You can do this either at the beginning of the day or the end of the day. You can be thankful for things as simple as the weather, a surprise phone call or message, your home, your health, your family, the green grass, a white blanket of snow, etc. Whatever strikes you as something you can be thankful for, write it down.

2. What is one thing about my spouse that I am thankful for today?
When you are in serious conflict (as you might be right now), you may not find it easy to find something to be thankful for in the moment. If that is the case, go back to the past and come up with something from your dating days or the earlier parts of your marriage. Go as far back as you need to and write down a topic of thanks. Here some basic examples to get your memory going: That time he/she made breakfast for me; when he brushed the snow off my car; when we walked hand in hand from school; that surprise gift; his/her faithfulness in taking care of the laundry; etc.

Order your copy of *The Unbreakable Marriage Gratitude Journal* at www.thesams.ca/resources or scan the following QR code.

4. READING THE BIBLE

> *"Your word is a lamp unto my feet and a light unto my path"* (Psalm 119:105).

Find a Bible reading plan and stick to it! Read a couple of verses or a couple of chapters, but regardless of what you choose, read your Bible everyday.

What is your Bible reading plan? _____

5. LISTENING TO SCRIPTURE

"Faith comes by hearing and hearing by the word of God" (Romans 10:17).

Download the Marriage Blessing audio recording (available at www.thesams.ca/resources) and listen to these faith-building scriptures each day.

Write down any scriptures that really stood out for you as you listened to the recording.

6. SHARING SPIRITUAL INSIGHTS

Take time to share with your spouse:

1. Any pictures, words, thoughts you received during your soaking time.

2. Specific reasons for gratitude that you wrote down in your Gratitude Journal.

3. Any revelations you wrote down while reading Scripture.

7. PRAYING IN AGREEMENT

"Truly I tell you that if two of you on earth agree about anything they ask for, it will be done for them by my Father in heaven" (Matthew 18:19).

Take time together to:

- Write down some reasons for thanksgiving that you would include in prayer today.

- Write down requests on your hearts.
    - Needs of others

    - Your personal needs

- Write down the declarations you are making and symbolically pull them down from heaven.

- Seal them with the Lord's Prayer:
    Our Father who art in heaven,
    Hallowed be Thy name.
    Thy kingdom come,
    Thy will be done,
    On earth as it is in heaven.
    Give us this day our daily bread.
    And forgive us our trespasses,
    as we forgive those who trespass against us.
    And lead us not into temptation, but deliver us from evil:
    For Thine is the kingdom, and the power, and the glory, for ever and ever. Amen.

8. REFRAINING FROM THE 4 C'S

Don't **C**riticize, **C**omplain, **C**ondemn, **C**ompare

- Decide to start refraining from the "4 C's" RIGHT AWAY.

- Give your spouse permission to catch you in the act of Criticizing, Complaining, Condemning and Comparing. We have a lot of fun with it. Whenever one person slips up, the other person says with a smile: "4 C's!"

- For an added incentive, throw a dollar (or more) in a jar every time you violate one of the "4 C's" with a touch of negativity. Treat yourself to something you enjoy with the loot you accumulate, or give away the money to a charity of your choice at the end of the week.

- Don't be discouraged if you encounter massive fails when you first get started on this. Old habits die hard…but the good news is that they do die eventually, if you keep on starving them.

How are you going to help each other stick to this spiritual discipline? What incentives (if any) are you incorporating?

_____

_____

_____

9. BLESSING YOUR SPIRIT

Look each other in the eye for 30 seconds straight. This might seem like an eternity when you first try it, but it gets easier. (You're allowed to blink, but the way)

For the MORNING, offer this blessing:

"_____ (name), I bless your spirit to rise up and walk hand in hand with Holy Spirit all through the day."

For the EVENING, offer this blessing:

"_____ (name), I bless your spirit to receive all that Holy Spirit releases to you all through the night."

How did you feel as you blessed each other's spirit?

_____

_____

_____

10. MAKING DECLARATIONS

*"Death and life are in the power of the tongue,
and those who love it will eat its fruit"* (Proverbs 18:21).

Each day, make these declarations based on I Corinthians 13:4-8.

Declare this over yourself:

"I am patient, I am kind. I do not envy, I do not boast, I am not proud. I do not dishonour others, I am not self-seeking, I am not easily angered, I keep no record of wrongs. I do not delight in evil but rejoice with the truth. I always protect, always trust, always hope, always persevere. My love never fails."

Make this declaration about your spouse. Substitute their first name in the blanks and read this aloud:

"_____ is patient, _____ is kind. _____ does not envy, does not boast, is not proud. _____ does not dishonour others and is not self-seeking. _____ is not easily angered and keeps no record of wrongs. _____ does not delight in evil but rejoices with the truth. _____ always protects, always trusts, always hopes, always perseveres. _____'s love never fails."

How did you feel as you made these declarations over yourself and your spouse?

_____

_____

_____

CHAPTER 3: SHIFTING THE SPIRITUAL ATMOSPHERE

REFLECTION

Which spiritual habits do you already practice?

_____

_____

_____

Which ones are you most looking forward to starting?

_____

_____

_____

Which ones will require a bit more effort on your part?

_____

_____

_____

_____

Daily Habits Produce Lifelong Results

One simple way to stay on track is to use a spreadsheet. For couples in our Marriage Mentorship Process, we set it up online so we can monitor how consistent they are. You can just as easily set up an offline spreadsheet, print it out and check off the boxes manually. A tracker is available at the back of this workbook.

Regardless of how you choose to track it, you will see the most effective and lasting change by setting up some form of accountability. Choose an accountability partner, a mentoring couple, or someone other than your spouse who will "hold your feet to the fire" and help you stay on track. This is one of the keys to producing breakthrough in your marriage. Without taking this step of accountability, you are much less likely to experience the kind of results couples have experienced by following this process.

1. Set up your Accountability Sheet.

2. Who are some couples or individuals you can ask to be your Accountability Partners? When and where will you meet? How often? Write out your plan below.

_____

_____

_____

_____

_____

CHAPTER 3: SHIFTING THE SPIRITUAL ATMOSPHERE

HOW TO SHIFT THE SPIRITUAL ATMOSPHERE SWIFTLY

Remember: HOLY SPIRIT, COME! Recall a time when you needed an immediate atmosphere shift. What happened? What difference could inviting the Holy Spirit have made?

_____

_____

_____

_____

_____

_____

_____

_____

_____

_____

CHAPTER 3: SHIFTING THE SPIRITUAL ATMOSPHERE

NOTES

CHAPTER 3: SHIFTING THE SPIRITUAL ATMOSPHERE

NOTES

CHAPTER 4:

REMOVING SPIRITUAL BLOCKAGES

CHAPTER 4: REMOVING SPIRITUAL BLOCKAGES

THE REAL ENEMY

"For our struggle is not against flesh and blood, but against the rulers, against the authorities, against the powers of this dark world and against the spiritual forces of evil in the heavenly realms" (Ephesians 6:12).

"You cannot win a spiritual battle with physical weapons. Spiritual battles call for spiritual weapons and spiritual strategies." - Jeeva and Sulojana Sam

TAKING THOUGHTS CAPTIVE

The first strategy we use is this: *"...bringing every thought into captivity to the obedience of Christ"* (2 Corinthians 10:5 NKJV).

You begin by first shifting the spiritual atmosphere. Remember those three powerful words? Say them now: "Holy Spirit, come!" Next you use this simple tool.

The H.A.L.T. Method

Hold that thought!
Arrest that thought.
Lock it up in a cell with Jesus.
Thank Jesus for taking care of that thought.

What situation are you facing right now where you can apply this strategy? Describe the situation and how the H.A.L.T. method helped.

_____

_____

_____

_____

CHAPTER 4: REMOVING SPIRITUAL BLOCKAGES

FORGIVING OTHERS

As you went through the teachings on what Forgiveness is not and what it is, what new insights or revelations (if any) did you receive?

_____

_____

_____

_____

_____

Forgiving From The Heart

"Forgiving from the heart takes seriously the effects of a person's hurt upon our entire being." - Jeeva and Sulojana Sam

Ask: "Holy Spirit, who do I need to forgive? What injustices have been done to me that I am still holding on to?" Write down every name without questioning any that God brings to your attention.

_____

_____

_____

CHAPTER 4: REMOVING SPIRITUAL BLOCKAGES

Pick one person from the list at a time, and ask the Holy Spirit to show you the effects of their actions upon you. Be honest with yourself about what you have lost as a result of what they did (or didn't do).

What emotions and feelings have I experienced as a result?

_____

_____

_____

What effects (if any) did this hurt/trauma have on my body?

_____

_____

_____

What lies have I been believing as a result of this hurt?

_____

_____

_____

What response(s) have I made, including making inner vows? Which of these might be distortions of God's will for my life?

_____

_____

_____

Pray as follows:

1. _____ (name), I give you the gift of my forgiveness. You owe me nothing. I choose to forgive you for _____ (what they did).

2. _____ (name), I choose to forgive you for the effects of your hurt(s) upon me.

3. I renounce the lies I believed and the inner vows I made. I repent of all ungodly responses to the way you hurt me.

4. Thank you, Father, for setting me free from all the effects of this hurt in every part of my being.

5. I ask you now to bless _____ (name) with_____ (what they need—peace, health, finances, job, business, salvation of loved ones, harmonious relationships, etc.)

You can also use a Scriptural blessing for your offender, such as this passage from Numbers 6:24-26 NKJV:
> "_____(name), *The Lord bless you and keep you. The Lord make His face shine upon you and be gracious unto you. The Lord lift up His countenance upon you and give you peace.*"

Repeat these steps for everyone the Holy Spirit highlights.

REPENTING OF JUDGEMENTS

Take some time now and ask God to show you anyone you have judged in the past, as well as who you may still be judging today. Write down every name that He brings to mind:

_____

_____

_____

_____

Then pray:

"Father, I do not want to reap judgment and condemnation against me by the judgments I have sowed against anyone. You alone are the righteous judge. I give up my right to judge others. I repent of the sin of judging _____ *(list all names the Holy Spirit brought to mind)*. I repent of judging them with my words, in my thoughts and in my heart. I ask you to forgive me and set me free from the consequences of my sin. I also ask you to cause those harvests of judgment to wither, dry up and die, so that they can produce no more fruit."

Take a moment to receive the forgiveness God offers, and then continue:

"I thank you, Father, for forgiving me and removing all judgments and condemnation that I had invited into my life. I praise you that none of these judgments will ever again boomerang in my face and prevent me from experiencing my breakthrough. In Jesus' mighty name. Amen."

CHAPTER 4: REMOVING SPIRITUAL BLOCKAGES

FORGIVING YOURSELF

You may already be aware of some things for which you have not fully forgiven yourself. Write them down.

_____

_____

_____

Go ahead and pray, "Holy Spirit, what all do I need to forgive myself for?" Write down whatever you receive in response.

_____

_____

_____

Pray, "What judgments (if any) have I made about myself as a result?"

_____

_____

_____

CHAPTER 4: REMOVING SPIRITUAL BLOCKAGES

Then offer this prayer:

"Lord, I choose today to give myself a gift of my own forgiveness. _____(your own name), I forgive you for _____ (read your list). I let it all go. I will not beat myself up about it anymore. I release it to you, Lord Jesus. I cannot be the Saviour for myself. Lord, you are my Saviour. I repent for making judgments about myself such as _____ (list all that Holy Spirit showed you). God, I ask you to forgive me and set me free from the consequences of my judgments."

Take a moment to receive His forgiveness. If these judgmental thoughts return, practice being compassionate to yourself and reminding yourself that no matter what happened, you were probably doing the best you knew how to do at the time, and you have decided to leave the matter with Jesus.

FORGIVING GOD

Pray:

"Holy Spirit, will you reveal to me all instances where I have blamed you for what happened in my life?" Write them all down:

_____

_____

_____

Then pray:

"Lord, I have blamed You for things that have happened to me and the circumstances of my life, such as _____. Today I am choosing to stop demanding an explanation before I can move on. You are a good God and someday I will understand a bigger picture that I cannot comprehend right now. I confess that holding this blame against you is wrong. I repent and ask you to forgive me. I release all my questions to you and today I choose to trust. I thank you for your patience and limitless love and I accept your mercy and grace. In Jesus' name. Amen."

Take a moment to receive His forgiveness and peace. How does that feel?

_____

_____

_____

_____

Whew! You've just completed some powerful processes in the spirit realm and removed several spiritual blockages preventing your breakthrough. Let us keep going till we take care of every possible impediment to intimacy with God that we are aware of.

CHAPTER 4: REMOVING SPIRITUAL BLOCKAGES

BREAKING OFF UNGODLY TIES

Pray:

"Holy Spirit, will you show me the people with whom I have an ungodly, unhealthy spirit, soul or bodily tie all through my life? Whether caused by their sin or my sin, please highlight these people to me." Write down each name.

_____

_____

_____

_____

Then pray:

"In the name of Jesus, I break off all unhealthy and ungodly spirit, soul or bodily ties that were established between me and _____ (names), whether in my mind, through my will, emotions or my body. God, I ask you to free me from any evil perpetrated by others. I repent for any way I have contributed to these ties being established myself. I release to the other person any part of them that remains in me that is rightfully theirs, cleansed by the blood of Jesus. I repossess any part of me that remains in them that is rightfully mine, cleansed by the blood of Jesus. Because you are the God of redemption, I declare that what the enemy meant for harm, you will turn to good as I walk in obedience to you in the days ahead. Thank you for restoring and making me new by your power. Holy Spirit, come now and seal this restoration you have done in my spirit, soul and body. In Jesus' name. Amen."

If you still have any objects in your possession that remind you of the person with whom you established this tie (e.g. love letters, journals, cards, gifts, jewelry, charms, clothing, etc.), we strongly suggest you get rid of them, so they do not continue to reinforce any unhealthy, ungodly, spirit, soul, bodily tie that may have been established.

BREAKING OFF GENERATIONAL HINDRANCES

What generational hindrances are you aware of in your family line? Write them all down. Consider both your father's and your mother's generational lines. Go as far back as you possibly can. You may need help from your parents, grandparents or other family members to compile this list.

_____

_____

_____

_____

Here is a prayer that you can use to break off all ungodly generational hindrances:

"In the name of Jesus, and by the power of His blood, I now break off all generational hindrances I have inherited from all my ancestors known to me, such as _____ (list them all) and others that are unknown to me. I place the cross of Christ between me and the sins of my ancestors. In the name of Jesus, I command all demonic oppression that has come down my ancestral lines to end right now. And I take back every generational blessing that has been withheld from me. Holy Spirit, come now and set your seal of freedom upon me and my future generations. In Jesus' name. Amen."

PARENTAL BLESSING

Since this could be a key element that contributes to breakthrough in your marriage, we urge you to find a way to receive a parental blessing.

The best option is for your birth father and mother or adopted parents to bless you. Feel free to use the blessings (pdf) from www.thesams.ca/resources or scan the following QR code.

The next best option is for your spiritual father/mother or pastor or mentor to release it to you.

If neither of the above in an option for you, feel free to use the audio recordings available at the website listed above.

Who can you ask for a parental blessing? What steps will you take to receive a parental blessing?

_____

_____

_____

_____

CHAPTER 4: REMOVING SPIRITUAL BLOCKAGES

ALIGNMENT

Our pastors Matt & Lisa Tapley preached a message called "Bold Love." We suggest you go listen to that audio here: www.thesams.ca/resources (or scan the QR code on the previous page) and then answer the following questions:

Father God
↓
Jesus
↓
Husband
↓
Wife
↓
Children

1. What points stood out as you listened to the recording? What did Holy Spirit highlight for you?

_____

_____

_____

2. The Tapleys mention many expectations God has of husbands and wives. Compare what you heard on the recording with what you saw in your parents' marriage. How did they model this for you positively?

_____

_____

_____

Where did they miss the mark?

_____

_____

_____

3. Now examine how those expectations are reflected in your own marriage. Where are you right on target with God's expectations?

_____

_____

_____

Where are you missing the mark?

_____

_____

_____

List some practical steps you could each take to ensure that your marriage reflects God's alignment.

_____

_____

_____

Share your responses with each other.

GOING DEEPER

Seek out a reputable team of inner healing ministers from any of the ministries we have mentioned at the back of this book, or others recommended by your pastor. If you'd like us to help you find a team, please reach out to us directly (again, see details at the back of the book).

Seek out a qualified professional Christian therapist. Many therapists can be found at www.psychology.com and www.psychology-today.com.

After receiving inner healing, take time to reflect on the experience. In what areas did you receive healing? What truths did the Holy Spirit reveal to you?

_____

_____

_____

_____

_____

What further healing/therapy do you need? Who can you seek to receive it?

_____

_____

_____

_____

CHAPTER 4: REMOVING SPIRITUAL BLOCKAGES

NOTES

CHAPTER 5

GROWING IN COMMUNICATION

CHAPTER 5: GROWING IN COMMUNICATION

LEVELS OF COMMUNICATION

Go through these questions that are designed to help you grow in your communication. Allow a few days or a week in between each set of questions. One person begins by reading a question and then listens intently without interrupting while the other person answers. You can ask them to clarify anything that is not clear to you once they have finished. Do not challenge or critique their responses.

Starter Questions

- If you won an all-expenses-paid trip to anywhere in the world, where would you go? Why?

- What are your favourite worship songs, hymns or choruses? Why are they your favourites?

- If you could meet anyone in the Bible, who would it be? Why? What would you ask them?

- What is one question you want God to answer? Why this one?

- Who are your heroes or people you have looked up to over the years? What makes them special to you?

- Describe two of your favourite memories of things we have done together.

Next Level Questions

- How are you like your Dad? Your Mom?

- How are you different from your Dad? Your Mom?

- What other relatives were important to you growing up? Why?

- What is something you have never done that you would like to try? Why?

- What is something that scares you that you would never ever try? Why?

- What is on your "bucket list"?

- Imagine your life 10 years from now. What excites you about growing older? What scares you about it?

LEVELS OF COMMUNICATION

Deeper Questions

- What are you really excited about right now? (Personally, in the family, work/business, church, country, etc.)

- What are you really scared about right now in the same areas?

- Share something new you have learned recently (about God, yourself, your spouse, family, work/business, the world)

- Share any dreams you have had during the night recently that you would consider significant. Do you have any idea what they might mean?

- Who in our family and friendship circles are you concerned about? How shall we pray for them?

- If you have received personal prophecies, listen again to any recordings you may have or read any written records/transcriptions. Which prophecies can you see becoming reality? Do any of them sound too good to be true? What changes do you need to make to partner with the Holy Spirit in making these words come true?

*** Don't forget to use Active Listening! ***

What did you learn about your spouse as you went through the levels of communication?

_____

_____

_____

Anything surprise you about the process?

_____

_____

_____

CHAPTER 5: GROWING IN COMMUNICATION

TRANSPARENCY

- Use the timeline on the following page to create a Life Line. On the far left edge enter "0" to mark your birth. At the far right edge, enter your current age.

- Ask the Holy Spirit to highlight key events that have shaped your life—both highs and lows. Mark high points above the line and low points below the line. High points might include significant events, achievements, what you are proud of accomplishing, graduation, marriage, jobs, the birth of a child, etc. Low points might include disappointments, failures, moves, breakup, divorce, hurts, losses. Do not hold anything back.

- Write a couple of words to describe each point and mark your age/year at each of the high & low points.

- Draw lines connecting the points (see illustration below)

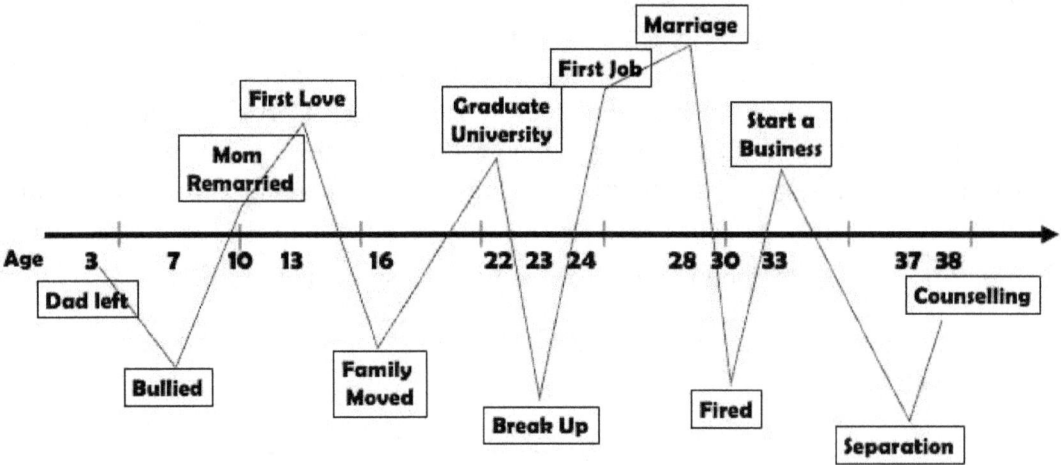

Share with each other the details of every item on both the upper and lower portions. As your spouse shares, respond with active listening. Ask questions for clarification. Be careful not to judge them. Remember, the goal is total transparency with empathy and compassionate, non-judgmental listening.

Celebrate the positives and celebrate God's grace and favour that were evident in those events. Share any unresolved hurts that remain from any of these memories/events. Help each other receive healing using the tools in the previous section for removing spiritual blockages as necessary. Seek out professional help should you need deeper healing.

You will be amazed by how transparency increases intimacy in your marriage!

CHAPTER 5: GROWING IN COMMUNICATION

LIFELINE

Birth

53

CHAPTER 5: GROWING IN COMMUNICATION

PHRASING YOUR HURT WELL

Transparency also requires you to communicate your hurts to your spouse. How do you do this? There are two key phrases that need to be part of this communication: "When you…" and "I felt…"

Two things happen when you phrase your hurt this way:
1. Your spouse now knows exactly what they did that hurt you. You are being transparent. You are pointing it out to them, but you are doing so in a way that does not accuse or condemn.

2. You are letting them know how you felt as a result of their hurt. When someone tells us how they are feeling, we should never tell them that they should not feel that way. The best response is to acknowledge their feeling before we do anything else.

If you have trouble finding the right "feeling" words, consult the Feelings Chart on the next page. You may also download a pdf of this chart at www.thesams.ca/resources or by scanning the following QR code:

Keep on practising what we have shared in this segment, and you will keep on growing in communication with each other.

CHAPTER 5: GROWING IN COMMUNICATION

CHAPTER 5: GROWING IN COMMUNICATION

Think of a time when you felt hurt by something your spouse said or did. What words from the Feelings Chart best describe how you felt? Be specific!

_____

_____

_____

_____

How could you phrase your hurt using those words?

When you…

_____

_____

I felt…

_____

_____

FURTHER COMMUNICATION

Wedding Day Memories

Find your wedding album or photos from your wedding day. Go through them together. If you have a video/movie, you can watch it as well. Enjoy reliving the memories of that day. Complete these sentences as you share from your heart with each other.

1. When I gazed into your eyes that day, I felt…

___

___

___

2. Some of the thoughts that went through my mind were…

___

___

___

3. The most memorable thing for me about our wedding was…

___

___

___

CHAPTER 5: GROWING IN COMMUNICATION

4. The funniest memory I have about our wedding day is…

_____

_____

_____

5. What I miss in our marriage today that we had on our wedding day is/are…

_____

_____

_____

6. How did it feel to share your wedding day memories together?

_____

_____

_____

Sharing Your Gratitude Journal

Find the Gratitude Journal that you have been keeping since you began this process. Share with each other every answer you have written to the question: "What is one thing about my spouse that I am thankful for today?" Look each other in the eye as much as possible during this sharing.

One spouse begins by reading all the reasons from their journal. Then the other spouse shares all their entries. Overwhelm each other with gratitude.

You can weave them into a prayer at the end, if you would like, such as,

"Lord, I thank you for _____.

I thank you that he/she _____."

How did your spouse respond to your Gratitude Journal? How did that make you feel? Share with them any entries that particularly delighted or surprised you.

_____

_____

_____

How did it make you feel to hear all the reasons for which your spouse is grateful for you? Share with them any entries that particularly delighted or surprised you.

_____

_____

_____

CHAPTER 5: GROWING IN COMMUNICATION

NOTES

CHAPTER 6

RESTORING PEACE FOLLOWING CONFLICT

CHAPTER 6: RESTORING PEACE FOLLOWING CONFLICT

> **CALL A TIMEOUT**

When might you need to call a timeout? How will it help the situation?

_____

_____

_____

_____

> **THE PROCESS OF RESTORING THE PEACE**

1. Begin in the spirit realm, asking and receiving forgiveness from God first. Then privately release forgiveness to your spouse.

2. Next move to the soul realm where you face your spouse in person, admit the hurt you caused, acknowledge the feelings aroused by it and ask them to forgive you.

3. Finally, involve both the soul & the body realm in coming up with a written plan to ensure that the issue behind the conflict is dealt with constructively.

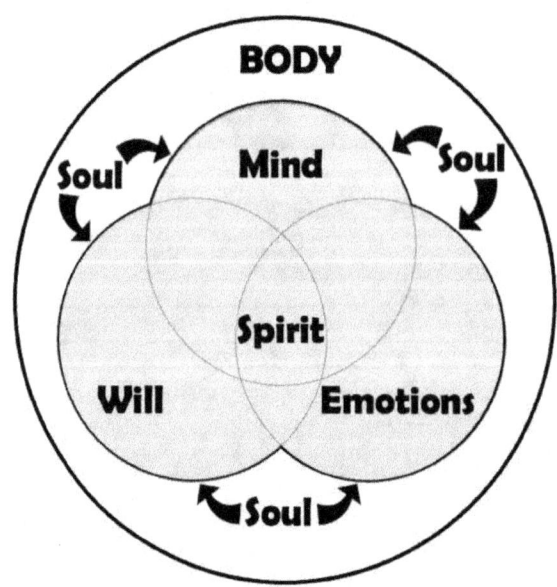

CHAPTER 6: RESTORING PEACE FOLLOWING CONFLICT

THE PROCESS OF RECONCILIATION

Here are the five elements of the process of reconciliation that you can apply to your conflicts.

1. Take responsibility:
- State exactly what you did that hurt your spouse. "I hurt you by..."
- Check with your spouse to make sure you got it right. "Did I get it right?"
- Change your statement of hurt according to their feedback. Do not question what they say (except for clarification). Do not justify or make excuses for what you did.

2. Show empathy:
- Make a sincere attempt to enter into your spouse's pain. Identify the feelings aroused by the hurt. Use the Feelings Chart, if necessary.
- Share with them the feelings you identified. "This is how you must have felt…"
- Check with your spouse for feedback on what you shared: "Did I identify all your feelings? Did I leave anything out?"
- Acknowledge any additional feelings they may share.

3. Express remorse:
- Share with them how you feel about hurting them. "I feel…"

4. Request forgiveness:
- "Will you please forgive me for what I did and the hurt it caused you?" Receive your spouse's forgiveness.

5. Commit to change:
- "These are the changes I will make to prevent this hurt from recurring." List them.
- Ask your spouse for feedback. "Is there any other change you would like me to make?" Agree to incorporate those changes into your commitment as well.

Make a list of all the hurts your spouse has caused you that remain unhealed.

_____

_____

_____

Use this Process of Reconciliation to receive your healing.

CHAPTER 6: RESTORING PEACE FOLLOWING CONFLICT

A PATTERN OF RESOLUTION

Work through an issue that remains unresolved in your marriage, even after going through the Process of Reconciliation.

Step 1: Meet In The Right Place…

_____

Step 2: … At The Right Time

_____

Step 3: Name The Issue You Are Resolving

_____

_____

Step 4: Examine Yourself First Before Blaming The Other. Ask: What role did I play that contributed to this problem?

_____

_____

Step 5: List All Possible Solutions Together

_____

_____

_____

_____

Step 6: Evaluate The Options and Agree On A Solution

_____

_____

Step 7: Follow Up Date to Evaluate

_____

Step 8: Our Reward as We Make Progress

_____

_____

How will implementing this pattern make a difference in your marriage?

_____

_____

After using the pattern listed above, reflect on how it went. What was positive? What can be worked on for the next time?

_____

_____

_____

You can download templates of the Process of Reconciliation and the Pattern of Resolution at www.thesams.ca/resources or by clicking the QR code below:

CHAPTER 6: RESTORING PEACE FOLLOWING CONFLICT

A RITUAL OF RECONCILIATION

Read 1 Corinthians 13:4-7.

You will notice there are 15 attributes of love listed in these verses. Substitute "I" for "love," and read each attribute out loud. Ask yourself: Does it ring true for me? How much of the time? How would my spouse grade me on this aspect of love?

Use the grid below to rate yourself on a scale of 1-10 for each attribute, where 1 is "Rarely or Never," and 10 is "All the time."

	1	2	3	4	5	6	7	8	9	10
I am patient										
I am kind										
I do not envy										
I do not boast										
I am not proud										
I do not dishonour others										
I am not self-seeking										
I am not easily angered										
I keep no record of wrongs										
I do not delight in evil										
I rejoice with the truth										
I protect										
I trust										
I hope										
I persevere										

- Ask God to forgive you for those attributes where you graded yourself at 5 or below.
- Ask your spouse to forgive you for those ways in which your failure to exhibit this characteristic of love has impacted them adversely. Be as specific as possible.

> Get a basin of warm water and a towel. Read John 13:1-15, where Jesus washes the feet of his disciples and tells them, *"Now that I, your Lord and Teacher, have washed your feet, you also should wash one another's feet."* Wash each other's feet—slowly, deliberately—as if to wash off the hurts that you confessed. Follow whatever directions the Holy Spirit gives you to experience and express that reconciliation.

Take a moment and reflect on the impact of the experience both on your heart and your connection with your spouse.

_____

_____

_____

_____

_____

_____

_____

_____

CHAPTER 6: RESTORING PEACE FOLLOWING CONFLICT

NOTES

CHAPTER 7

GOING UNDERCOVERS

CHAPTER 7: GOING UNDERCOVERS

TRANSPARENCY & EMOTIONAL CONNECTION

Here is a common list of trust matters than can cause either spouse to hold back sexually:

- Withholding something financially

- Battling an addiction that they are not willing to admit

- Committing a sin they are not willing to confess

- Hiding something from their past that they are ashamed of

- Keeping any other kind of secret

Does anything in this list resonate with you? What are some things you need to be more transparent about with your spouse?

_____

_____

_____

_____

How can you connect emotionally with your spouse more?

_____

_____

_____

_____

CHAPTER 7: GOING UNDERCOVERS

IMPROVING YOUR SEXUAL CONNECTION

Affection And Appreciation Outside The Bedroom

If you take inventory of all that you say to your spouse in a typical day…
How much of your talk would be classified as affectionate?

_____

_____

How much would be classified under one of The "4 C's" (Criticizing, Condemning, Complaining and Comparing)?

_____

_____

Ask your spouse: Would any of my words qualify as put-downs, defamation, or calling you by unflattering names?

_____

_____

_____

Ask your spouse: Which words do I use that make you feel sexy, admired, appreciated?

_____

_____

_____

How much would be simply conveying information?

_____

_____

_____

How much would be "giving orders" or more "To-Do List" type talk?

_____

_____

_____

CHAPTER 7: GOING UNDERCOVERS

Ongoing Communication

What are some things your spouse does sexually that are pleasing to you, and which are not?

_____

_____

_____

Performance Anxiety

How can you relate to the concepts of "orgasmic pressure" and "organic pleasure?" What changes do you need to make to take pressure off your spouse and add sexual pleasure?

_____

_____

_____

Physical Considerations

Ask your spouse:
What are your preferences for personal hygiene that I am not meeting right now? What changes do I need to make?

_____

_____

_____

How does my level of fitness affect our sexual connection? What changes do I need to make? What can both of us do to become more physically fit?

_____

_____

_____

Are any of your health issues affecting us sexually? How are you addressing them positively?

_____

_____

_____

The Plague Of Pornography

If pornography is part of your life, share how it is affecting you.

_____

_____

How is it affecting your spouse?

_____

_____

What steps are you taking to become porn-free?

_____

_____

_____

CHAPTER 7: GOING UNDERCOVERS

GUIDELINES FOR SEXUAL CONNECTION

Here are the guidelines we share in the book:

- Prioritize sex in your schedule.
- Allow room for spontaneity.
- Connect emotionally with each other more frequently than you connect sexually.
- Connect physically every day with gestures of affection that do not necessarily lead to sex, such as hugs, kisses, caresses, sensual touch, or whatever else your spouse enjoys.
- Remove all hindrances standing in the way of you giving yourselves to each other, before you initiate the sexual connection.
- Prepare yourselves as best as you can physically so you can give yourselves to each other unreservedly. Eat healthy foods, exercise regularly, take care of health issues and maintain the standard of personal hygiene your spouse expects of you.

Which of these guidelines do you need to adopt? How would you apply them practically to improve your sexual connection?

_____

_____

_____

_____

_____

_____

_____

CHAPTER 7: GOING UNDERCOVERS

GOD WANTS YOU TO ENJOY SEX

How does this statement affect the way you view our sexual connection? Did you grow up believing this truth? What other beliefs did you grow up with? How are they impacting our sex life?

_____

_____

_____

_____

Read the Song of Solomon in its entirety and write down verses/phrases that stand out for you.

_____

_____

_____

_____

_____

Weave some of them (as they are or in your own words) into compliments you can offer your spouse.

CHAPTER 7: GOING UNDERCOVERS

NOTES

CHAPTER 8

MAKING TIME

CHAPTER 8: MAKING TIME

A COMMON CALENDAR

1. Look at your calendar for this month.

2. Set aside weekly blocks of uninterrupted time to be together first (minimum 3 hours, if possible).

3. Block off all children's activities that require your presence (if any).

4. Mark all your working hours/scheduled business time slots.

5. Block off time for exercise, sleep and periods of rest.

6. Enter your time apart to pursue your individual interests/hobbies.

7. Go back and make any adjustments required to ensure that your calendar reflects your priorities.

8. Decide together what you will do with the rest of the available free time (if any).

By following these steps, you will make sure that you are making time in your marriage for the people who matter the most to you, beginning with each other.

List your activities and schedule considerations below.

_____

_____

_____

_____

_____

CHAPTER 8: MAKING TIME

How will you incorporate "Our Night/Date Night" into your calendar? Which time slot can you set aside consistently?

_____

_____

_____

What are some leisure activities that you enjoy doing together?

_____

_____

_____

What do you enjoy doing by yourself only?

_____

_____

_____

Use the blank calendar on the next page to plan out a sample month.

CHAPTER 8: MAKING TIME

Month:

Sunday	Monday	Tuesday	Wednesday	Thursday	Friday	Saturday

NOTES

CHAPTER 8: MAKING TIME

NOTES

CHAPTER 9

MARITAL FINANCES

CHAPTER 9: MARITAL FINANCES

KEY CAUSES OF FINANCIAL STRESS

Circle any points of financial stress that exist in your marriage due to:

- Different philosophies
- Established patterns
- Underlying beliefs
- Not having enough income
- Debts
- No written budget
- No written goals
- Lack of transparency

What are your personal beliefs, philosophies and patterns about finances? How do they align with your spouse's?

_____

_____

_____

_____

_____

_____

Do you have a written budget? _____

Is there enough income coming in? _____

What are your debts?

_____

_____

_____

What steps can you take to get out of debt?

_____

_____

_____

What financial "secrets" (if any) do you need to disclose to each other?

_____

_____

_____

_____

CHAPTER 9: MARITAL FINANCES

What do we want our retirement to look like? Where will we live? What will we be doing with our time?

_____

_____

_____

If we have a mortgage, when do we want to be mortgage-free? What will being mortgage-free feel like? What will it do for us?

_____

_____

_____

What kind of vacations do we want to take? All-inclusive? Cruises? Oceanfront? Cottage life? Wilderness hikes? Skiing?

_____

_____

_____

If we have excess cash, what do we want to invest in? Real Estate? Stocks and bonds? Cryptocurrency? Precious metals? Other assets?

_____

_____

_____

CHAPTER 9: MARITAL FINANCES

ELIMINATING FINANCIAL STRESS

Here are the guidelines we share in the book to help eliminate financial stress:

- Find a financial consultant or mentor – we recommend Dave Ramsey
  www.ramseysolutions.com

- Set up a monthly written budget - Free download available at
  www.ramseysolutions.com/budgeting/useful-forms

- Do at least one mid-month check-up to assess how you are doing

- Establish a maximum personal spending limit for each spouse

- Have joint bank and credit card accounts

- Honour God with your tithes and offerings

CHAPTER 9: MARITAL FINANCES

Which of these guidelines can you follow to help you address the causes of financial stress you identified earlier?

_____

_____

_____

What areas do you need to seek help from a professional?

_____

_____

_____

Who are some people you can contact to get the help you need?

_____

_____

Who did you decide to work with?

_____

When will you get started?

_____

CHAPTER 9: MARITAL FINANCES

NOTES

CHAPTER 9: MARITAL FINANCES

NOTES

CHAPTER 10

BOUNDARIES

CHAPTER 10: BOUNDARIES

TRIANGULATION

Triangulation is when a husband or a wife allows a third party to enter their marriage and form a triangle. This could potentially result in the strangulation of the marriage. You could say that triangulation is the combination of a triangle + strangulation.

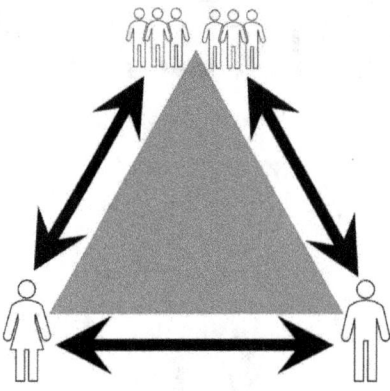

List any instances of triangulation in your marriage—past and present:

_____

_____

_____

_____

Share them with each other. Use the process of reconciliation and the pattern of resolution from earlier, as necessary.

BOUNDARIES FOR YOUR MARRIAGE

Go through the list of boundaries in Chapter 10 of the book. Write down which of these you need to set up to protect your marriage.

_____

_____

_____

_____

_____

_____

_____

_____

CHAPTER 10: BOUNDARIES

What more would you add to the list? Why?

_____

_____

_____

_____

_____

What boundaries do you think Jesus had?

_____

_____

_____

_____

Why are boundaries healthy and necessary?

_____

_____

_____

CHAPTER 10: BOUNDARIES

NOTES

CHAPTER 10: BOUNDARIES

NOTES

CELEBRATE YOUR UNBREAKABLE MARRIAGE

1. How do you plan to celebrate completing the process of making your marriage Unbreakable -- with a special meal, getaway, etc.? Where will you celebrate?

_____

_____

_____

2. If you are renewing your marriage vows…

Who will be the officiant?

_____

Where will this take place?

_____

Which vows will you be using?

_____

Here are the traditional vows:
In the presence of God and before these witnesses,
I, _____, take you, _____, again, to be my wife/husband, to have and to hold from this day forward, for better for worse, for richer or poorer, in sickness and in health, in joy and in sorrow, to love and to cherish, and to be faithful to you alone, as long as we both shall live (till death us do part). This is my solemn vow.

Don't forget to kiss each other right after!
Your officiant may use the blessing on the next page or declare other words of blessing over you.

A BLESSING FOR YOUR MARRIAGE

"May the Lord cause you to flourish, both you and your children. May you be blessed by the Lord, the Maker of heaven and earth"
(Psalm 115:15-16).

May you:
Love, honour and cherish each other,
work together with one mind and purpose;
forgive as the Lord forgave you and live in unity as one flesh.

"May the God of peace make you holy in every way, and may your whole spirit and soul and body be kept blameless until our Lord Jesus Christ comes again"
(1 Thessalonians 5:23).

*"The Lord bless you and keep you.
The Lord make His face shine upon you and be gracious unto you.
The Lord lift up His countenance upon you and give you peace"*
(Numbers 6:24-26 NKJV).

AFTERWORD: WHERE DO YOU GO FROM HERE?

Congratulations on working your way through this workbook! Reading *"The Unbreakable Marrriage"* coupled with what you have done in this workbook may be all you need for you to receive breakthrough in your marriage.

Some of you, however, still need more in-depth help to help you get there. If that's you, we would highly recommend that you receive personal, customized mentorship with us or another mentoring couple we have trained, over 12 weeks. This includes weekly sessions, mid-week checkups, unlimited inner healing sessions and 24/7 access to your mentors via email and text. 3 monthly follow-ups thereafter are also included. Results guaranteed or money back (conditions apply). By application only at www.thesams.ca .

We invite all of you to join our free Facebook group "The Unbreakable Marriage Community" where you can interact with other readers of this book and encourage one another. We will also be posting more teachings, updates and information on exclusive events you can attend to take your marriage to greater heights in that group.

Just click on: http://www.facebook.com/groups/theunbreakablemarriage/ or scan the barcode below:

ACCOUNTABILITY TRACKER

Accountability Tracker

Date																
1. Soaking																
2. Praise & Worship																
3. Gratitude																
4. Bible Reading																
5. Scripture Audio																
6. Insight Sharing																
7. Praying Together																
8. The 4 C's																
9. Spirit Blessing																
10. Declarations																

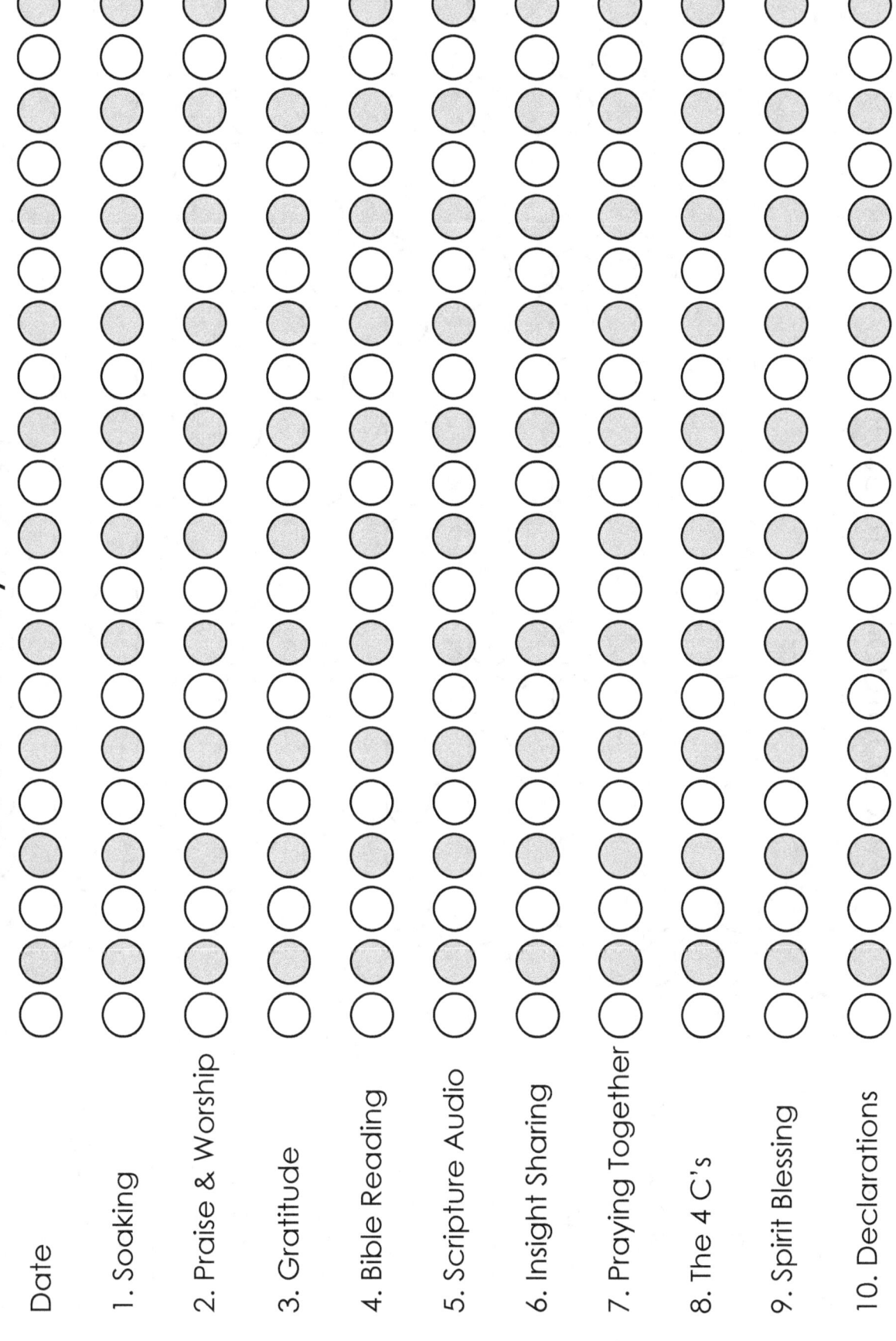

Accountability Tracker

Date																	
1. Soaking																	
2. Praise & Worship																	
3. Gratitude																	
4. Bible Reading																	
5. Scripture Audio																	
6. Insight Sharing																	
7. Praying Together																	
8. The 4 C's																	
9. Spirit Blessing																	
10. Declarations																	

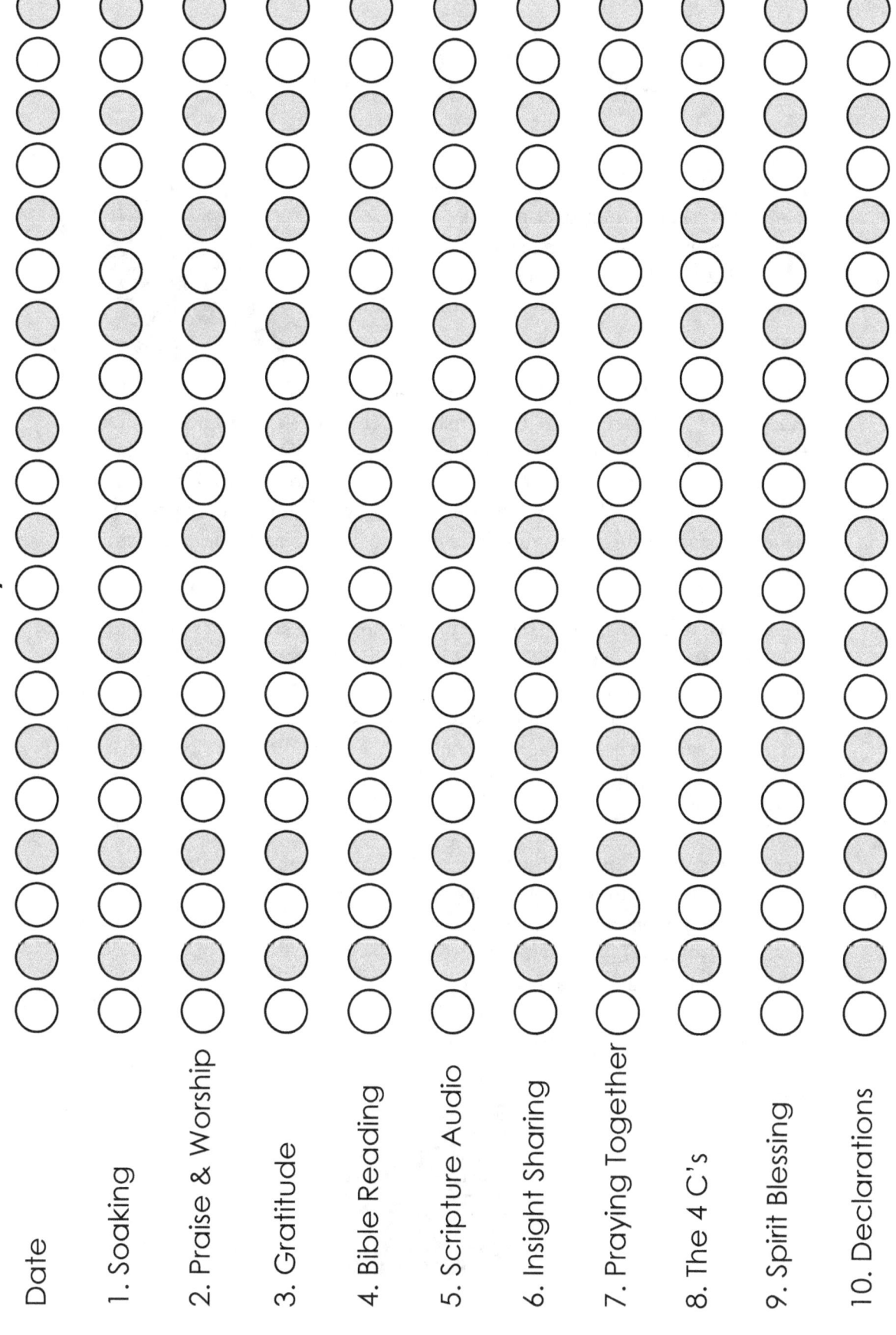

ABOUT THE AUTHORS

JEEVA AND SULOJANA SAM are marriage mentors based in Ontario, Canada. Jeeva retired in 2017 after 35+ years as a pastor. Sulojana has worked for the Government of Canada since 2007. They reside in the Niagara Region of Canada.

The Sams are celebrating the 39th anniversary of their arranged marriage in 2022. They are parents of three married children--Priya and her husband, Duncan, Sathiya and his wife Shaloma and Jaya and his wife Rachel. They were one of three couples featured on 100 Huntley Street's 40 Day Love Dare Challenge in 2010. This experience eventually led them to create a process which guarantees breakthrough for couples facing breakdown in as little as 10 weeks.

The Sams strongly believe that no matter how broken a marriage may be, it can be restored when BOTH husband and wife commit themselves to do whatever it takes to make it work. Once they learn how to access the power of God, apply the sound biblical principles and use the tools in this book, they are certain to turn their marriage around. Jeeva and Sulojana are on a mission to save 50,000 marriages from divorce in the next 5 years. Your marriage could be one of them!

Reach out to them and get the help you need by visiting www.thesams.ca
or by e-mail: theunbreakablemarriage@gmail.com.
Connect with them on social media:
Facebook: @theunbreakablemarriagebook
Instagram: @theunbreakablemarriage

Join The Unbreakable Marriage Community at
www.facebook.com/groups/theunbreakablemarriage or by scanning this QR code:

www.ingramcontent.com/pod-product-compliance
Lightning Source LLC
Chambersburg PA
CBHW081710100526
44590CB00022B/3725